The author (left) undergoing the type of painful and useless treatment that she suffered a few years ago; (above) the author today.

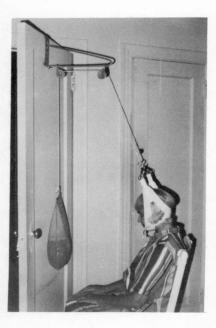

PAIN-FREE
ARTHRITIS

BY
Dvera Berson

WITH
Sander Roy

DRAWINGS BY
Wendy Frost

SIMON AND SCHUSTER • NEW YORK

DESIGNED BY EVE METZ
MANUFACTURED IN THE UNITED STATES OF AMERICA
2 3 4 5 6 7 8 9 10

LIBRARY OF CONGRESS CATALOGING IN PUBLICATION DATA

Berson, Dvera.
    Pain-free arthritis.

    1. Arthritis.   2. Pain.   3. Hydrotherapy.
4. Exercise therapy.   I. Roy, Sander, joint author.
II. Title.
RC933.B48   616.7′2   78-520

ISBN 0-671-24042-0

CONTENTS

THIS BOOK IS DEDICATED TO MILTON AND JOYCE, WITHOUT WHOM MY LIFE AND THIS BOOK WOULDN'T HAVE BEEN POSSIBLE.

Introduction

Dvera Berson has developed her own unique program of exercises for the treatment of arthritis pain, by means of hydrotherapy. I don't mean that she invented hydrotherapy as a useful program, for exercising in water has been an aspect of arthritic treatment in special places and institutions for years. However, my observation of patients who have gone to spas invariably has shown a consistent improvement, but a transient one. Once the patient returned home, he or she relapsed into a usual pattern of activity and any temporary improvement was quickly lost.

The value of superexercise has been clearly demonstrated for a patient with a long history of mixed arthritis, but to the best of my knowledge it has never before been extended to the superperiods of time practiced by Dvera Berson, and defined in this book. To do what she has accomplished requires patience, tolerance, and motivation. She has all of these qualities, and the almost miraculous improvement in her entire physical well-being has been the most ample reward for the effort and determination she puts into her program. I use the word "puts" in the present tense because, as the author clearly points out many times in her book, the program must continue to be carried on, probably throughout life, or else the good effects are vitiated. Though Dvera Berson has shown this tremendous improvement, it is not entirely unexpected since her exercise program makes a great deal of medical sense. Not only does it treat the cause of arthritis pain, but it does so in a program that a motivated patient can follow without undue strain.

While Dvera Berson's superexercise program may well be the first truly helpful innovation in physical therapy of arthritis in the past hundred years, it cannot and does not claim to be a cure, but it is certainly the next best thing I have ever witnessed in all my years of affiliation with the Arthritis Foundation and with the Arthritis Clinic at Maimonides Hospital. This intensive course of hydrotherapy and exercise helps to improve muscle function, restore muscle strength and improve the strength of ligaments and bones. This program will reverse many of the sad consequences of arthritis. Today Dvera is an active, remarkably strong and happy person after years of crippling misery, and although she has to continue to work regularly at her exercises she has come to enjoy them and would not give them up even if she could.

The improvement in Dvera's physical well-being is also naturally reflected in her return to a healthy emotional state. She no longer has severe depression and anxiety, and the result is tremendously less need for toxic medications, tranquilizers, and antidepressants. Whenever a patient can dispense with or radically cut down on the use of toxic medication, arthritic management becomes simpler, safer, and less costly.

Dvera Berson's is a case history that may well turn out to be the guideline for more complicated and extensive programs in hospitals and in active arthritis groups of all sorts. Meanwhile her story and her exercise instructions must surely be an inspiration for any individual who suffers from this dreadful affliction and who now sees a proven way by which pain from arthritis can be banished.

B. JAGENDORF, M.D.

Preface

This is the true story of how I used *pain-free* special water exercises to conquer crippling arthritis. It tells how I used them to *gradually relax, stretch* and *strengthen* the muscles surrounding my joints and thus gradually eliminate all feelings of pain and stiffness from my body.

When I was sixty years old, I had been suffering from arthritis for six years and I was getting progressively worse. I wore a neck brace and a back support, slept in a hospital bed, did traction three times a day, had deformed fingers, and was in constant pain. My condition was diagnosed as being rheumatoid arthritis and osteoarthritis, osteoporisis and cervical spondylosis deformans. The way things were going, I was in very real danger of becoming permanently crippled, but I didn't stand by and let this happen to me. I did something about it.

Today, at age sixty-five, my pains are one hundred percent better and my fingers are no longer deformed. I sleep in a regular bed and no longer need back or neck support. I have progressed from being unable to sign my name without severe pain to being able to swim the backstroke 100–150 lengths of a pool, totaling up to a mile and a half.

I have medical records, doctor bills, X rays, blood tests, drug bills, and hospital records to document what my condition was. I tell you this because people meeting me today for the first time would never know that I had ever suffered from serious arthritis.

Today, the only limitations with my condition are that I can't lift heavy objects without some pain and that if I stop water exercising for two weeks I start to feel some pain and stiffness return to my hands and neck. Otherwise, when I keep up with my water exercises I can carry on all normal activities without any pain whatsoever.

What I accomplished was the result of a special program that I developed myself.

The Arthritis Foundation and most reputable arthritis doctors recommend proper exercise as being very beneficial in the treatment of arthritis. The problem with exercises that doctors recommend is that they are too painful to do for someone already in pain. I personally experienced this problem. In the first years of my illness, my internist sent me to a physiotherapist for arthritis exercises. The exercises that he gave me hurt me so severely that I was forced to discontinue them. The reason that I was able to persevere with my special water exercises is that they are absolutely pain free.

What they accomplished was to gradually relax, stretch and strengthen the muscles surrounding my joints. Over a period of weeks and months of relaxing, stretching and strengthening, my body became progressively less painful and more flexible. Eventually, all feelings of pain and stiffness were eliminated from my body.

Starting ten minutes a day with pain-free special water exercises, I changed my life. If you, or someone you care for, suffers from arthritis, you owe it to yourself to read this book.

Most people have come to accept their arthritis pain the way they accept death and taxes. They are very unhappy about the situation but feel there is little or nothing they can do about it. This book was written to announce that now there is something they can do about it, if they really want to.

The arthritis pain-relief program described in this book

PREFACE
does not involve changing your diet slightly, nor does it involve swallowing a new miracle drug. What it does involve is your expending effort to help yourself. The disadvantage of my special water exercise program is that it isn't an instant magic cure. The advantage is that it really works! That is the most important thing about this book. It offers people who want to help themselves the knowledge of how to really do it.

It is not my intention, though, to suggest this program as a replacement for a patient's doctor. Hopefully, this program will be of help to both doctor and patient in treating the patient's arthritis pain. The self-help aspect of this book comes into being because doctors do not have pools in their offices and they don't have the time to go to pools to supervise and encourage the individual exercise programs of every one of their patients.

General exercise principles are repeated on a separate page in special type every now and then throughout the twenty-five beginner's-exercise descriptions. I risked boring you with such repetition only because of the importance to you of understanding why these principles have to be emphasized. If you do not pay strict attention to them, the rest of the program will be rendered ineffective.

The books I have read about arthritis fall into two categories: quack books that offer simple, easy solutions that don't work, and legitimate general-information books that tell you everything about arthritis except what you should do about it. This book is a legitimate attempt to help you help yourself. I tried to treat you not as a nameless patient but rather as a sensitive human being who happens to be in a lot of pain. I tell you about my own suffering and recovery to inspire you to achieve your own recovery. This book does not attempt to be a general-information book about arthritis. I have tried to include only information that would be of direct benefit to you in improving your condition.

DVERA BERSON

The reason I'm smiling is that I no longer have to wear these monstrosities. In my right hand I'm holding the surgical corset I wore around my lower back. In my left I'm holding the collar I wore around my neck. Draped over my left arm is the back support I wore around my upper back.

By the way, that was my third cervical collar; I wore out the first two.

It's nice to be able to dress like this without having to wear a cervical collar.

The best thing about this picture is that I'm standing straight. That doesn't seem like much, but standing straight was something I was unable to do for quite a few years.

Contrary to some rumors, there are times when I get out of the swimming pool.

Exercise 34 is my modification of the conventional Olympic-style backstroke, which is designed for maximum speed. Mine is designed for maximum pain relief to the back and neck.

Here I am in the whirlpool at an indoor health club. Remember, you won't be smiling if you stay longer than 3 minutes.

I call this Exercise 35 "the wiggle." When I do it for 45 minutes, swimming most effortlessly, I move each of my shoulders, arms, legs, and hips approximately 2,200 times.

This is Exercise 31. To receive the greatest benefit from it, be sure your arms and legs do not merely skim the water. They should push the water forcefully, first toward you and then away from you.

My Life Before

What follows is a brief history of what I suffered physically and mentally before my life changed for the better.

I didn't think it could happen to me, except that it did. I always thought arthritis was something that happened to "old people." When this all started I was fifty-four and I didn't consider myself old. I didn't know what arthritis was doing bothering me. In fact, at first I didn't even know I had arthritis.

It started with a pain in my jawbone, for which I naturally went to a dentist. I felt relieved when my dentist couldn't find anything wrong with my teeth or gums.

The pain persisted and so did I. I went to my internist, who gave me Indocin for my jaw. After a few weeks the pain went away and I thought no more about it.

Six months later, seemingly out of nowhere I developed excruciating pains in my neck, back, hands and the lower back of my head. This all happened over one terrible weekend. My internist told me I had arthritis. He put me on a program of taking eight Bufferins a day.

On one of my subsequent visits, when I complained about the pain, my doctor told me, "You have to learn to live with it." That statement convinced me to change doctors. Even at that stage, when my pains were a lot less than they were to become, there was no way I could learn to live with them.

I decided to get expert advice, so I called the Arthritis Foundation. They recommended an arthritis clinic not far from where I lived. At the clinic, they took X rays and blood tests, both of which confirmed that I had rheumatoid arthritis, osteoporosis and osteoarthritis. I went to this clinic for about three months. The doctors there prescribed medication for me which did not help at all.

After this, on the recommendation of a friend of mine, I went to an internist who made every effort to help me— first with cortisone and then with two series of gold treatments. When I was taking these treatments my pains stopped getting worse and were, in fact, about twenty-five percent better. The unfortunate thing about both cortisone and gold is that, because of harmful side effects, you can take only a limited number of shots before being forced to discontinue the treatment.

After five and a half years of various treatments, my neck got so bad that it was decided to put me in the hospital for supervised traction. I had twenty-one days of Blue Cross coverage, so that was my allotted time for recovery. As it was, I had only three days of traction. It turned out that I was lucky this happened, because the traction I received for three days was the opposite of the kind I needed.

I found this out by going to an orthopedic surgeon affiliated with a different hospital. After a thorough examination he, at least, prescribed a way to give me outpatient traction that helped rather than hurt my condition. After a few months of correct traction my neck improved to the point where the pain was awful but bearable. The pain was especially bearable since the surgeon had told me that the only alternative to enduring it was having an operation on my neck.

Over a six-year period, because of cortisone and gold treatments and probably because of the natural course of the disease, my condition didn't decline in a straight line. I had "good" periods as well as "bad" periods. The problem with my "good" periods was that they seemed good only when compared to my "bad" periods. I was always in pain. Also in each succeeding "good" period my condition was worse than it had been in the previous "good" period.

My condition declined down a series of plateaus rather than in a straight line, but over a period of time the decline was nevertheless relentless. After six years of spending countless money and effort to help myself, I had "improved" to the point where I was wearing a neck brace and a back support and doing over-the-door traction three times a day. My hands were crippled and I was in constant pain.

MY MENTAL AND EMOTIONAL CONDITION

I wish I could say that during my trials and tribulations with doctors and hospitals I always kept my head high and my spirit strong. Not true. First of all, I couldn't keep my head high. Physically, my condition was such that I had to walk with a stoop. Unfortunately, my mental and emotional condition matched my physical condition.

Aside from the pain, the hardest thing to live with was not having any hope for recovery. I am a fairly strong person, and I think I could have endured anything if I had known that at some point my suffering would end and I would survive. After a while it looked as if the only time my pains were going to stop was when I stopped existing.

When my first internist told me, "You have to learn to live with it," my first reaction was one of defiance. I said to myself, "What does he know? I'll find a doctor who can help me." Three years later my reaction was quite different when I showed a doctor in whom I had more confidence the three fingers on my right hand that were gnarled and deformed and giving me excruciating pain. I asked, "Doctor, do I have to wait to undergo this torture with every finger?" He replied, "That's a very difficult question to answer." That answer depressed me as much as the pain.

There I was, going to the best internist I could find, doing everything he said, and on a year-to-year basis I was worse every year. It got to the point where I would lie in my darkened bedroom and just cry to myself without tears, "Why me?" My condition was so bad that I wasn't ever physically comfortable. I used a cervical pillow when lying in bed, but even that didn't help. I couldn't lie for more than ten minutes at a time without having to change my position.

I had the same problem trying to sit for more than ten minutes at a time. There was a two-hour waiting time at my doctor's office. I had to spend the two hours alternating between sitting for ten minutes and standing for ten minutes with my back leaning against the wall for support.

Before all this happened to me, I was a divorcée with hopes of remarriage but with no one special in mind. Afterward, one of the things I would think about in my darkened room was, "Who would want me now?" While I still hoped to be married to someone I could care for, that marriage could take place only in a world now hopelessly lost to me—a world where my pains and deformity didn't exist. The way things really were, I had no interest in any people, male or female. As I retreated into myself, everyone else's problems and concerns seemed very petty to me. The only reality was me and my pain.

While I am admitting other unpleasant thoughts that I had at the time, let me admit that I was also ashamed of myself. I wasn't ashamed of feeling sorry for myself or being involved with myself to the exclusion of everything else. Rather, I was ashamed of being a cripple.

In the winter I could hide my hands with gloves. I always wore my back support under my clothes. What I couldn't stand was having to wear my cervical collar in public. I told casual acquaintances that my collar was for a pinched nerve. I told strangers who met me for the first time that I was suffering from whiplash.

In general, I can say that my mental and emotional condition was one of frustration, unhappiness and very little hope. In my darkened room, the thing I thought of most was that my life was over.

Looking back on my six years of suffering, I think my state of depression helped contribute to the worsening of my condition. It was a vicious circle. Being tense, nervous, and unhappy caused my muscles to be tenser and tighter, which in turn caused me more pain. This in turn caused me to be even more tense and nervous. At the time, I was dimly aware of the situation, but there was nothing I could do about it.

As long as I was in constant pain and without real hope, I found it impossible to think happy, positive thoughts. Once I started doing my water exercises and felt tangible physical improvement, I found it a lot easier to maintain a positive attitude. Once happy thoughts became based on happy realities, I found them much easier to come by. I always strongly believed in positive thinking, but I found it impossible to think positively when I was living in a world filled only by pain and hopelessness.

My Exercise History

In the six years that I spent waiting for someone else to help me, I was treated by two internists and two physiotherapists, consulted with an orthopedic surgeon, was hospitalized for traction, used a hydrocollator for my neck and parafin for my hands and also received cortisone injections and two series of gold injections, plus countless oral medication. None of these treatments proved to have any lasting benefit.

The only treatment that has ever provided me with complete and lasting relief is my muscle-relaxing water exercise program.

As of this writing, I have absolutely no pain. I can proudly walk with my head up. I don't wear a cervical collar or use a back support or do any traction. I don't take drugs or visit doctors for arthritis. My fingers are no longer deformed.

The principle of exercising in water is a simple one. Movement is much easier in water than out of it. On dry land every movement is a fight against gravity. In the water, you are lighter and more mobile, because your body is being supported by the buoyancy of the water. Exercises that cause pain and strain when done on dry land can become easy and pain free when done in the water.

I started my exercises at an outdoor pool, while I was on a three-month vacation in Florida. I have to admit that at the time I didn't have any grand design for curing myself. I had two main thoughts when I started. One was the hope of doing a little something to improve my condition. The other was the fear of doing something to hurt myself badly.

When I started, I was amazed at the freedom from pain I had when I moved. Even so, I confined myself to slow gentle movement and made sure to rest as soon as I felt the least bit tired. I exercised every day, and by the end of the first week I noticed some slight improvement. During the next three months I increased my stamina and flexibility by gradually lengthening the time I spent on each exercise and gradually increasing my radius of movement. What happened was that I was slowly loosening and relaxing my muscles, while at the same time strengthening them.

The obvious improvement in my physical condition, and the knowledge that it was because of something I myself was doing, gave me a tremendous psychological lift. Having hope for the first time in years definitely helped relax my mind. As I became more relaxed and less tense mentally, my muscles relaxed even more. I am sure that the interreaction of mental, physical and emotional improvement helped speed my recovery.

By the end of my three months in Florida, while I wasn't yet well, I was considerably better. My pains were much less severe. I had more general stamina and I had a much greater interest in doing things other than worrying about myself.

Unaccountably, when I returned to New York I didn't immediately continue with my water exercises. I can't remember exactly why. Possibly I thought I was permanently better. Possibly, I wasn't yet a hundred percent convinced that my exercises were the sole things responsible for my improvement. And possibly, after feeling better, I became lazy. In Florida, I could walk out of my hotel room and into the pool thirty seconds later. In New York, it's a lot more trouble to find and travel to a pool.

After being back in New York six weeks and seeing slow

changes for the worse in my condition, I remembered how much better I felt in Florida and made up my mind to join a health club. After two weeks there, my condition improved to the level it had been in Florida. It kept right on improving, and after a while I felt confident enough to start doing the backstroke. For my condition, this was the perfect exercise. In a relaxed position on my back I can exercise my wrists, arms, shoulders, neck, back, hips, and feet all in one motion. Even today, when I have no pain, I swim slowly and in a relaxed manner and pause at one end of the pool. My current regimen consists of forty-five minutes of doing the backstroke and one other advanced exercise, three minutes in the whirl-pool, and then forty-five minutes of the same exercises, fin-ishing with three minutes in the sauna.

Even though I have made tremendous progress in my con-dition, eliminating pain, swelling and deformity from my body, I am not cured. Recently I was on vacation in Cali-fornia, visting relatives. I was relaxed mentally. Physically I encountered no strain and enjoyed myself immensely, visit-ing, sight-seeing and eating out. Yet at the end of a pleasant month of not exercising in California, I felt stiffer and tighter throughout my body. I also had slight pains in my neck and hands.

Back in New York, after a week of exercising, my condition came back to normal. This further proved to me that I'm not cured, but rather involved in a lifetime discipline of helping myself.

How the Exercises

Work

As I've pointed out, this exercise program, even if done properly, will not cure you of arthritis. What it will do is effectively treat the symptoms of arthritis so that you can eliminate your pain and regain flexibility. Arthritis is a disease of the joints, but it is in the muscles surrounding the joints that you feel most of your arthritis pain and stiffness. Tense, tight muscles press on nerve endings. Weak and tense muscles make movement painful and difficult.

My special water exercise program treats your pain by treating your muscles. It gradually *relaxes, stretches* and *strengthens* tense, tight and weak muscles. Over a period of time as your muscles gradually relax, stretch and strengthen, your joints become progressively less painful and more flexible.

Since these exercises are virtually pain free, you don't have to worry about torturing yourself in the hope of seeing improvement. But you do have to have patience. You can't expect to exercise for one day, or one week, and see great improvement. These exercises will work for you, but they are not magic. After a few weeks you can expect slight improvement, and after a few months you can expect major improvement.

By doing these exercises regularly, you gradually increase the strength and flexibility of your muscles. If you don't do them regularly, all the benefit is lost. Every time you exercise, there is a slight, unnoticeable increase in muscle strength. Imagine your muscle strength as being 100 units of strength. After exercising one day, you build yourself up to 101 units of strength. If you exercise the next day, you start at 101 units and build yourself up to 102 units. If instead of exercising the next day you wait a few days, you would have to start all over again at 100 units of strength.

By exercising every day or at least five times a week, you build your strength and flexibility progressively. On a day-to-day basis, this increase will not be noticeable, but on a month-to-month basis your progress will be amazing.

Once you have achieved the desired results of eliminating your pain and increasing your flexibility, you can congratulate yourself. But you cannot retire from your exercise program. Remember, you have not cured yourself of arthritis. You have merely controlled the symptoms.

If you stop doing your water exercises, you will find your units of strength decreasing just as steadily as they increased before. Gradually, you will again become aware of discomfort and impaired movement. To prevent this from happening, you must continue doing your exercises three times a week as a maintenance program for the rest of your life.

Once you have seen the benefits of these exercises, and how enjoyable they are to do, you won't resent that fact. Instead you will love this regimen as much as I do.

A LITTLE INSPIRATION

It is very simple. If you want to help yourself you can. You don't have to endure pain and physical suffering. You don't have to endure the mental anguish of wondering how much worse you are going to get. You can look forward to a life free of pain and deformity. All you have to do is be willing to make a continuous effort to help yourself.

With my special water exercises you don't have to endure additional pain. You don't have to worry about hurting yourself. You can concentrate on helping yourself.

For the purpose of doing exercises beneficial to your arthritis condition, think of the water as the best friend you have. Any time you move any part of your body in the water, that movement is much easier and much less painful than the same movement on dry land. The buoyancy of the water makes your body feel almost weightless. Every movement is less of a strain. Exercises that are too painful to do on dry land can become pleasant to do when done in the water.

Don't take my word for it. Go to a pool and see for yourself. Without signing up for a long-term membership, ask to try the facilities, or pay for one day. Being careful to follow instructions, try the beginner's exercises illustrated in the next chapter that pertain to your condition. See for yourself how much easier they are to do in the water than out of it. Then prepare to dedicate yourself to helping yourself.

If you are willing to follow instructions and put in the required effort, you can change your life.

CONFIRMATION

Before you start reading the exercise section of this book I want to emphasize an important point. What I say about arthritis pain being caused by tense, tight and weak muscles is not just my pet theory to explain my recovery. That arthritis pain is felt in the muscles and caused by tense, tight muscles pressing on nerve ends is a medically accepted fact. It is also a medically accepted fact that weak and tense muscles make movement painful and difficult.

The popular misconception that arthritis pain is caused by deterioration of the bones is exactly that, a popular misconception. Deterioration of the bones and joints is certainly involved in arthritis but is only occasionally the direct cause of arthritis pain. Tense, tight and weak muscles are the direct cause of almost all arthritis pain. Once you accept that fact you can easily accept the thesis that effectively treating your muscles will reduce and eliminate your arthritis pain.

The special water exercise program you will read about in the next chapters does effectively treat your muscles. By adhering to this program I dramatically changed my life for the better. You can do the same.

CHRONIC BACK AND NECK PAIN

My special water exercise program should be very beneficial to many people who suffer from chronic back and neck pain not involving arthritis. First check with your doctor to determine the cause of your pain. Then ask your doctor if effectively treating your muscles and ligaments would reduce your pain. There is a strong likelihood that it would.

While tense, tight and weak muscles are not responsible for everything bad in this world, they do play a major part in causing most chronic back and neck pain. Simply put, the problem is that your muscles are not strong enough to properly support your skeletal system. Conservative treatment suggests wearing cumbersome surgical corsets and cervical collars to provide added support for your back and neck. My program suggests gradual strengthening of your muscles so that they can perform their natural function without the need for collars and corsets.

I have two reasons for mentioning chronic back and neck pain in a book supposedly devoted exclusively to arthritis. The first is their similar common cause of pain. The second is my wish that people suffering from chronic back and neck pain should achieve a similar happy result from their treatment.

General Information about
the Exercises and Exercise Facilities

1. If your problem is arthritis of the fingers, wrists, toes or ankles, you can derive benefits from doing my water exercises at home in your bathtub. Arthritis of the elbows, shoulders, neck, back, hips and knees requires a larger body of water to work in. Climate permitting, these exercises can be done in an outdoor pool or the ocean. To exercise the year round in a city, as is my case in New York, you have to find access to a pool.

2. Using an indoor pool doesn't have to be an expensive proposition. In addition to health clubs, organizations like YMCA's, YWCA's, schools and religious organizations have pools. The health club where I belong gives a fifty percent discount to people over sixty-two and does not ask proof of age. Before signing any contracts try the various facilities at least once and inquire about discounts. Do not let yourself be pressured to your disadvantage by aggressive salesmen. Also, there is precedent that, if your doctor prescribes this program for you, the Internal Revenue Service may well allow the costs as a medical deduction you can take on your income tax.

3. It is very inconvenient to have to go to a pool five times a week, but that inconvenience is nothing when compared to the good it does. I travel back and forth by bus, and I don't enjoy waiting for buses, especially in the winter. I find, though, that whatever inconvenience and discomfort this brings is a thousand times better than being in pain. The same rationale applies to the expense involved in joining and traveling to a health club. I find that by spending money to join a pool, I'm saving a fortune in doctor and drug bills.

4. The water in the pool doesn't have to be any particular temperature, as long as it doesn't feel chilly. Also the air temperature in the area around the pool shouldn't be colder than the water. Even today, with my condition a hundred percent better, I never swim in cold water or take cold showers.

5. When I started doing my water exercises, I did the exercises every day, weather permitting. This was because I was very enthusiastic about them, and because traveling to the pool was no problem. If traveling or other commitments make everyday exercise inconvenient for you, five times a week is the acceptable minimum to start with. Once you have achieved your desired goals, a maintenance program of three times a week is sufficient to prevent relapse. If it is a physical impossibility for you to get to a pool five times a week, you are better off going three times a week than not going at all. If you start three or four times a week you will definitely improve. The only drawback is that your improvement won't be fast, and it may or may not be as complete.

6. When I say that these exercises are pain free I mean that they do not cause any additional pain. That doesn't mean that your pains will miraculously disappear as soon as you enter the water. What it means is that properly exercising in the water causes no more pain than being motionless on dry land.

Exercise that does cause increased pain not only is uncomfortable but also is bad for you. Increased pain causes increased muscle tightness, which in turn causes even more pain. Exercise without increased pain is good for you because it causes muscles to relax and stretch, and thus reduces your pain. That is why exercise that causes increased pain should be avoided, and exercise that doesn't should be encouraged.

The water makes exercise much easier to do. Exercising in

the water should not cause additional pain. If you do experience some additional pain it is because you are trying to do too much too soon. Lessen your exercise repetitions and/or range of motion. Find a level of exercise that is comfortable for you and then gradually build yourself up from there. If you do things moderately, you shouldn't experience any additional pain.

7. All my movements in the water are of a slow and gentle nature. The idea is to *relax, stretch* and *strengthen* the muscles, not strain them.

8. To exercise for an hour requires much more muscle strength than to exercise for five minutes. That is why you should always strive to increase the amount of time you spend exercising. You'll know you are doing enough in the water when you reach the point where on dry land, you are no longer in pain. When I started, I did each exercise for about a minute. My general rule was that when I was tired or felt any slight strain, I stopped and rested. In time, as I became more flexible and increased my general stamina, I was able to exercise for longer periods of time without feeling any additional strain. Increases in duration of exercise time didn't follow any preconceived plan. They followed naturally from the improvement of my condition.

9. When I started I didn't have the full range of movement to do most of the exercises completely. I didn't worry about it. I started doing them partially, and gradually built up my flexibility. Let me emphasize again that slow and gentle movements in the water lead to steady, gradual improvements in stamina, muscle strength and flexibility.

10. Nowhere in this book do I ever tell you to do an exercise for five minutes or to repeat it ten times. Each person's condition is different from everyone else's. The fact that I could do an exercise ten times when I began exercising has nothing to do with you. You might be able to do it thirty times, or only one time and then only partially. When you are exercising it is important that you do only as much as is comfortable for you to do and then try to improve from there. Improvement doesn't depend on how much you can do in the beginning. It depends on how much you persevere.

11. I make it a rule always to go to the pool at off hours, when it is least crowded. When I swim or do my other exercises, I'm very careful of other people. I don't want to injure anyone or be injured myself. Occasionally I find inconsiderate people who swim as if they are the only ones in the pool. I make it my business to watch out for them. I also pick out fixed points in the ceiling under which I will swim. That enables me to keep my course straight.

12. After I've finished my exercises, showered and dressed, I rest at least twenty minutes in the lounge before going home. I do this especially in the winter, to make sure that the cold outside air isn't a shock after the warmth of the pool.

13. The health club where I belong has a beautiful, well-equipped gymnasium. I manage to avoid it like the plague. To this day, I will not exercise on dry land. Why should I? If I try to demonstrate the twisting motion of the backstroke even once on dry land, I feel a slight strain. In the water, I can swim the backstroke for an hour without feeling any strain whatsoever.

14. At the halfway point in my exercises, I go into the whirlpool for three minutes. I sit with the water up to my chin. I also make sure to sit between the jets so that the force of the jets doesn't hurt me. The whirlpool isn't necessary for my exercise program, but it gives a pleasant and relaxing

sensation. After the whirlpool, I slowly reenter the pool and submerge myself up to my neck to readjust my body temperature. When I start to swim again, I start especially slowly so as to gradually get myself back into the rhythm of things.

15. A word of caution about the use of both the sauna and the whirlpool: stay no longer than three minutes in either one. On more than one occasion I have seen someone go into the whirlpool for the first time, spend fifteen minutes there, and then have to be carried out. By the way, from the arthritis standpoint, there is no reason for spending too much time in either the sauna or the whirlpool. Heat treatments of any sort temporarily relax your muscles but provide no permanent benefit.

16. If I have been on vacation or have had a virus or for some other reason have been unable to do my water exercises, for a week or two I do only eighty or ninety percent as much as I did the last time. Each occasion is different, but usually after a few sessions I'm able to work myself back comfortably to where I was.

17. This book outlines a self-help program that will help you greatly, but self-help does not mean self-diagnosis. Before starting this program I suggest you check with your doctor. If it hasn't already been done, your doctor can determine if you actually have arthritis. Just because you have pains that seem like arthritis doesn't necessarily mean that you have arthritis. Your doctor can also determine if you have some physical condition other than arthritis that might be adversely affected by this form of moderate exercise.

Here is a word of obvious medical caution. In one of the early stages of rheumatoid arthritis, some people develop a fever. If you have such a fever you should not attempt pool exercise. You should, however, discuss my special water exercise program with your doctor. He will tell you how soon after the fever subsides you can start an exercise program.

18. All exercise movement should feel as if you are *pushing* and/or *lifting* the water. When you get this feeling, it means that you are using the water to provide slight resistance to your movement. This resistance helps to increase your muscle strength.

19. The exercises are divided into beginner's, intermediate and advanced exercises. Start with the beginner's exercises appropriate to your condition. Some beginner's exercises should be replaced by intermediate and advanced exercises as soon as you are able to do so. Others do not have an effective intermediate or advanced replacement, so they must be continued. The procedure you should follow is noted under each beginner's exercise.

20. Don't worry about not being able to do the beginner's exercises. Before I started my exercise program, I hadn't exercised in over forty years. These exercises were specially written for the level of people who never exercise, and who additionally are in a great deal of pain.

21. Make sure you try to do all the beginner's exercises that apply to your condition, not just the ones you like best. These exercises are designed to be used in combination with one another, so as to put your muscles through their full range of motion and thus provide the maximum benefit for you.

Your First Day
of Exercise

Do not attempt to do too much. Your first day should be a testing process to determine what you can and cannot comfortably do. Try the various exercises that apply to your particular condition. Even if you find all the exercises easy, do not overdo any of them. If you do overdo an exercise, you might not feel badly in the pool but could experience increased discomfort within the following twenty-four hours. If this happens do not be discouraged, just wait a few days and then do much less the next time you exercise. Remember, your muscles are not used to exercise and they must be gradually built up.

If you experience increased discomfort from trying to duplicate the full range of motion pictured in a drawing, then only do the exercise partly. Make sure that you do all your exercise repetitions within a range of motion that is comfortable for you. In ensuing days and weeks try to gradually increase both your range of motion and the number of repetitions you do. Do not be discouraged if the drawing shows a thirty-six-inch range of motion and you can only move three inches comfortably. Keep trying and you will experience gradual progressive improvement.

When you are doing three or four exercises for a particular condition it is possible that one of them may be too uncom-

fortable for you to do even partly. If that is the case, then
don't force yourself to do it. Do the other exercises for a
month and then try the hard one again. If you still can't do it,
then try again a month later. Eventually the other exercises
will build you up to the point where you will indeed be able
to do the one or the ones that gave you difficulty.

It is much easier to exercise in water than on land. The
probability is that if you are careful you will not experience
any increased discomfort. If you do experience some discomfort the first day it is because you exceeded the limits of what
is comfortable for you to do. Sometimes that is unavoidable
because you can't know your limits until you test them. The
important thing, though, is to find a level of exercise that
is comfortable for you. Once you do that, the battle is almost
won. The rest is just a matter of gradual increases in range
of motion and number of repetitions. Remember, don't
overdo anything the first days or weeks. If you are content to
start slowly and improve gradually, you will be very satisfied
with your final result.

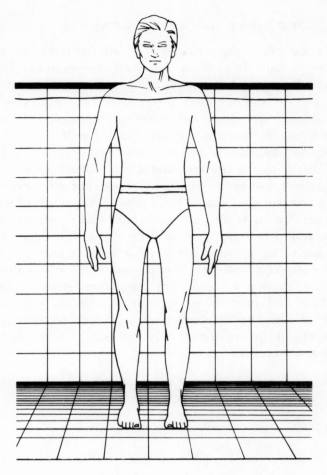

WHERE AND HOW TO STAND

When doing standing exercises for your arms, stand with
your back near the edge of the pool so that you don't have
to worry about careless swimmers colliding with your back.
When doing these exercises, make sure the water is always
above the part being exercised. If you are doing ankle exercises, but additionally have a problem with low-back pains,
stand in water well above the area of pain so that you get
maximum support for that sector while exercising your ankle.

Beginner's Exercises

The following instructions apply to each and every one of the twenty-five beginner's exercises.

Do an exercise for as long as you comfortably can without its becoming a strain. When you become tired, it is important that you stop and rest. After resting, repeat the exercise if you can.

In the beginning, if you can't even do any or all of these exercises for very long, or if you don't have the full range of movement pictured, it is important to have patience with yourself. In time your stamina and flexibility will increase naturally, and it will become much easier to do each exercise for longer periods of time with a greater radius of movement. The rule is always to try to do a little more than you did the last time, if you can do it without increasing the strain on yourself.

There is almost no benefit from doing these exercises once or twice a week. They should be done at least five times a week at the beginning. Then, once you have achieved your desired results, you can reduce to a three-times-a-week maintenance program. Remember, results take time.

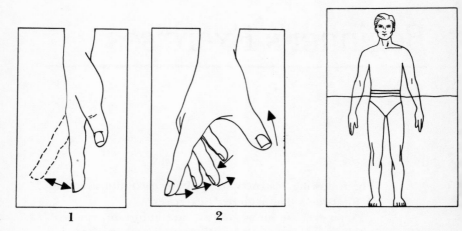

1   2

Exercise 1—To *relax, stretch* and *strengthen* the muscles surrounding your finger joints.

Stand in water to your waist with your hands comfortably at your sides as shown. Then flutter your fingers. Move each of your fingers forward and backward the way the one finger in Figure 1 is being moved. All your fingers should be moving at the same time, but they should be moving independently. As some fingers are moving forward others should be moving backward as shown in Figure 2. Notice that the thumb movement is up and down, not backward and forward. If you find this thumb movement awkward, don't worry about it. In time your thumb will more easily coordinate with the rest of your fingers. All finger movement should feel as if you are *pushing* the water. All movement should be *slow* and *gentle*.

This exercise quite possibly can be done at home in a bathtub or basin, but take note of the caution spelled out on page 84.

The exercise should be continued regardless of the advanced exercises you do.

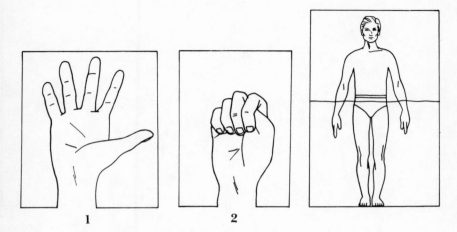

1   2

Exercise 2—Further to *relax, stretch* and *strengthen* the muscles surrounding your finger joints.

Stand in water to your waist with your hands comfortably at your sides as shown. With your palms facing toward your body, open each hand and stretch your fingers as much as you comfortably can, as shown in Figure 1. Then attempt to clench your fist as shown in Figure 2. All opening and closing motions should feel as if you are *pushing* the water forward and backward. All movement should be *slow* and *gentle*.

If you intend to do the exercise at home, see the caution on page 84.

This exercise should be continued regardless of the advanced exercises you do.

40

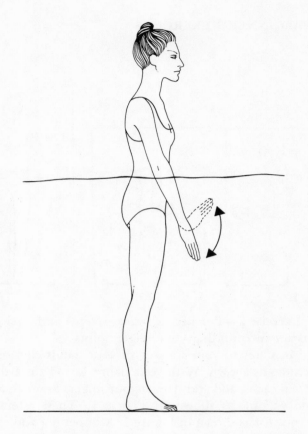

Exercise 3—To *relax, stretch* and *strengthen* the muscles surrounding your wrist joints.

Stand in water to your waist. Without raising your arm, raise your hand below the wrist as high as you can and then lower it as far as you can. All raising and lowering motions should feel as if you are *pushing* and *lifting* the water. All movements should be *slow* and *gentle*.

If you intend to do the exercise at home, see the caution on page 84.

This exercise should be replaced with Exercises 32 and 33 as soon as you are able to do so.

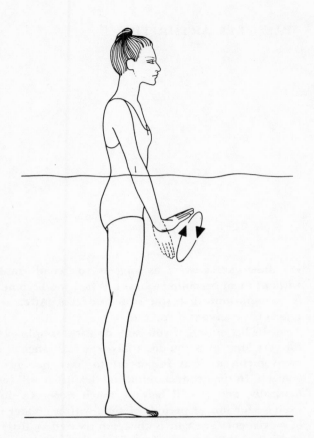

Exercise 4—Further to *relax, stretch* and *strengthen* the muscles surrounding your wrist joints.

Stand in water to your waist. Rotate your hand below the wrist so that you feel as if you are *pushing* the water around in a circular motion. Rotation should be to the right for a period of time and then to the left for a period of time. All movement should take place in your hand below the wrist. Try not to move your upper arm. All movement should be *slow* and *gentle*.

If you intend to do the exercise at home, see the caution on page 84.

This exercise should be continued regardless of the advanced exercises you do.

Do these exercises for as long as you comfortably can without them becoming a strain. When you become tired, it is important that you stop and rest. After resting, repeat the exercises if you can.

In the beginning, if you can't do these simple exercises for very long, or if you don't have the full range of movement pictured, it is important to have patience with yourself. In time your stamina and flexibility will increase naturally, and it will become much easier to do each exercise for longer periods of time with a greater radius of movement. The rule is always to try to do a little more than you did the last time, if you can do it without increasing the strain on yourself.

There is almost no benefit from doing these exercises once or twice a week. They should be done at least five times a week at the beginning. Then, once you have achieved your desired results, you can reduce to a three-times-a-week maintenance program. Remember, results take time.

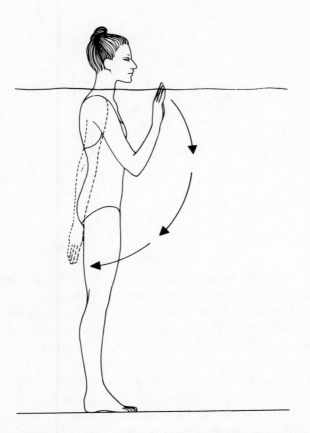

Exercise 5—To *relax, stretch* and *strengthen* the muscles surrounding your elbow joints.

Stand in water above your shoulders. Raise and lower your arm below the elbow so that on the raising and lowering motions you feel as if you are *lifting* the water up and *pushing* the water down. All movement should be *slow* and *gentle*.

This exercise should be replaced with Exercises 32 and 33 as soon as you are able to do so.

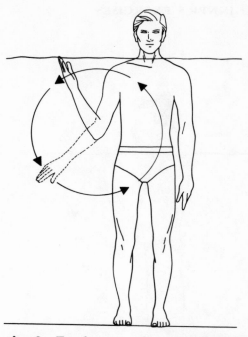

Exercise 6—Further to *relax, stretch* and *strengthen* the muscles surrounding your elbow joints.

Stand in water above your shoulders. Rotate your arm below the elbow so that you feel as if you are *pushing* the water around in a circular motion. (To complete the circle you will have to adjust the position of your elbow.) Rotation should be to the right for a period of time and then to the left for a period of time. Try to make sure most of the movement takes place below the elbow. Your shoulder should not move very much. All movement should be *slow* and *gentle*.

This exercise should be continued regardless of the advanced exercises you do.

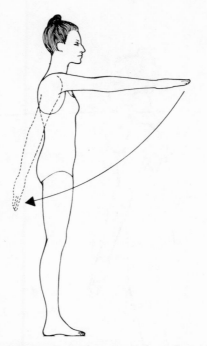

Exercise 7—To *relax, stretch* and *strengthen* the muscles surrounding your shoulder joints.

Stand in water to midneck. Raise and lower your arm so that on the raising and lowering motions you feel as if you are *lifting* the water up and *pushing* the water down. All movement should be *slow* and *gentle.*

This exercise should be replaced with Exercises 34 and 35 as soon as you are able to do so.

This exercise does not put your shoulder through its full range of motion, which is achieved only when this exercise is replaced with advanced Exercise 34. Exercise 34 is the best way of putting your shoulder through its first full range of motion.

If you cannot eventually do Exercise 34, then Exercise 7 may be modified to provide full range of shoulder motion. Stand in water to midneck and raise your arm above the water so that it is perpendicular to the water. Then lower your arm as shown in the drawing for Exercise 7.

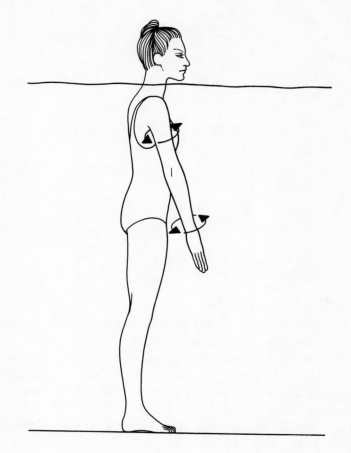

Exercise 8—Further to *relax, stretch* and *strengthen* the muscles surrounding your shoulder joints.

Stand in water to midneck. Rotate your arm so that you feel as if you are *pushing* the water around in a narrow circular motion. Rotation should be to the right for a period of time and then to the left for a period of time. All movement should be *slow* and *gentle*.

This exercise should be replaced with Exercises 34 and 35 as soon as you are able to do so.

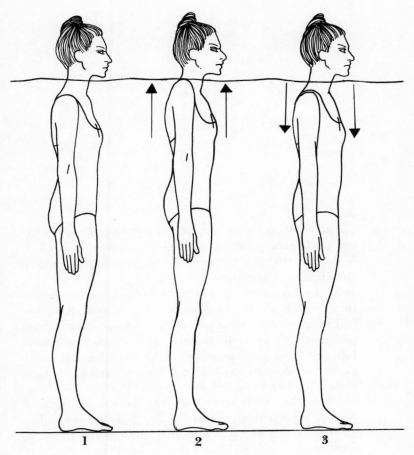

1   2   3

Exercise 9—To *relax, stretch* and *strengthen* the muscles surrounding your lower-neck, upper-back and shoulder joints.

Stand in water to midneck. Raise and lower your shoulders in a shrugging motion. The raising motion should feel as if you are *pushing* the water up. All movement should be *slow* and *gentle*.

This exercise should be replaced with Exercise 10 as soon as you are able to do so.

Do an exercise for as long as you comfortably can without its becoming a strain. When you become tired, it is important that you stop and rest. After resting, repeat the exercise if you can.

In the beginning, if you can't even do any or all of these exercises for very long, or if you don't have the full range of movement pictured, it is important to have patience with yourself. In time your stamina and flexibility will increase naturally, and it will become much easier to do each exercise for longer periods of time with a greater radius of movement. The rule is always to try to do a little more than you did the last time, if you can do it without increasing the strain on yourself.

There is almost no benefit from doing these exercises once or twice a week. They should be done at least five times a week at the beginning. Then, once you have achieved your desired results, you can reduce to a three-times-a-week maintenance program. Remember, results take time.

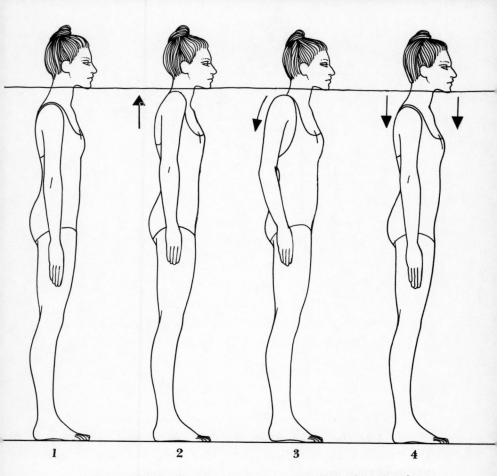

1	2	3	4

Exercise 10—Further to *relax, stretch* and *strengthen* the muscles surrounding your lower-neck, upper-back and shoulder joints.

Stand in water to midneck as shown in Figure 1. Raise your shoulders straight up as shown in Figure 2. Then rotate your shoulders with a backward circular motion and start lowering them as shown in Figure 3. Return to starting position as shown in Figure 4. The raising motion should feel as if you are *pushing* the water up. All movement should be *slow* and *gentle*.

This exercise should be replaced with Exercises 34 and 35 as soon as you are able to do so.

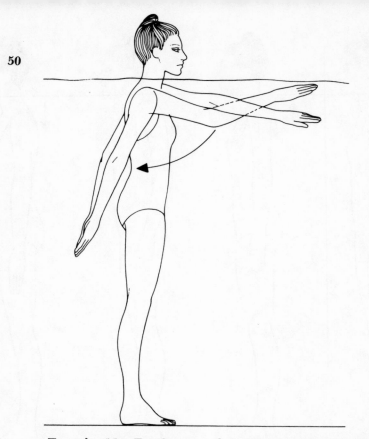

Exercise 11—Further to *relax, stretch* and *strengthen* the muscles surrounding your shoulder, lower-neck and upper-back joints.

Stand in water to midneck. Move your arms up and around in front of you so that you cross your elbows. Then move your arms as far back behind you as they will comfortably go. All arm motion should feel as if you are *pushing* the water forward and backward. All movement should also be *slow* and *gentle*.

This exercise should be replaced with Exercises 34 and 35 as soon as you are able to do so.

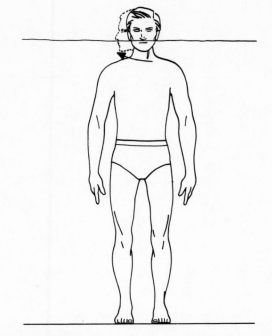

Exercise 12—To *relax, stretch* and *strengthen* the muscles surrounding your neck joints.

Stand in water just below your nose. Keep your mouth closed and breathe through your nose. It is important that you stand in water this deep so that the water will be able to support your neck. Turn your head as far as you comfortably can to the right and then return to center. Then repeat the same movement to the left. All movement should feel as if you are *pushing* the water. All movement should also be *slow* and *gentle*.

This exercise should be continued regardless of the advance exercises you do.

> **When doing this exercise be especially careful. If you feel the least bit dizzy, stop immediately. If you are in any way hesitant about being able to do the exercise safely, don't do it. Instead, concentrate on doing the lower-neck, upper-back and shoulder exercises, especially Exercises 10 and 11. Most of the neck muscles are connected to the upper back and the shoulders, and they can be successfully treated by effectively exercising those areas.**

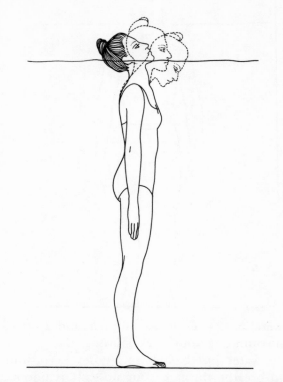

Exercise 13—Further to *relax, stretch* and *strengthen* the muscles surrounding your neck joints.

Stand in water just below your nose. Keep your mouth closed and breathe through your nose. It is important that you stand in water this deep so that the water will be able to support your neck. Lower your head as far as it will comfortably go toward your chest. Then raise it as far back as it will comfortably go. All raising and lowering motions should feel as if you are *pushing* the water down and *lifting* the water up. All movement should be *slow* and *gentle*.

This exercise should be continued regardless of the advanced exercises you do.

NOTE: The warning for the preceding exercise (page 51) applies to this one too.

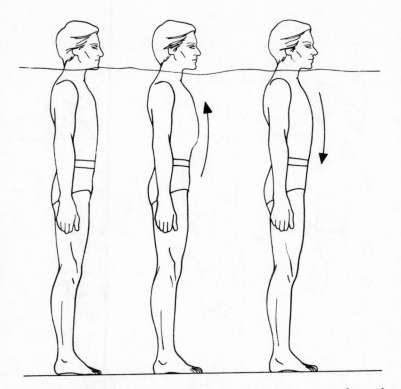

Exercise 14—To *relax, stretch* and *strengthen* the muscles surrounding your upper-back joints and to improve your posture.

Stand in water to midneck. Breathe in deeply, raising your chest. Hold the chest up, then exhale. All movement should be *slow* and *gentle*.

This exercise should be replaced with Exercises 34 and 35 as soon as you are able to do so.

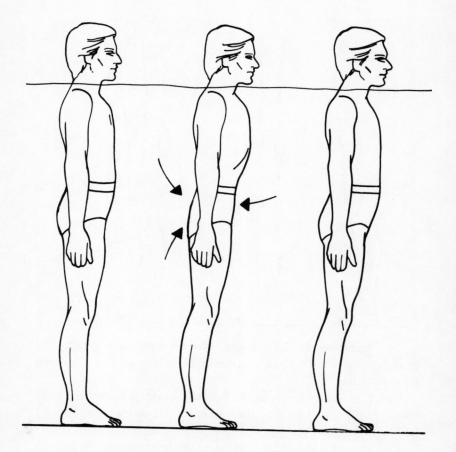

Exercise 15—To *relax, stretch* and *strengthen* the muscles surrounding your lower-back joints and to improve your posture.

Stand in water above your shoulders. Tighten your buttock muscles and pull in your stomach, then release. All movement should be *slow* and *gentle*.

This exercise should be replaced with Exercises 34 and 35 as soon as you are able to do so.

Do an exercise for as long as you comfortably can without its becoming a strain. When you become tired, it is important that you stop and rest. After resting, repeat the exercise if you can.

In the beginning, if you can't even do any or all of these exercises for very long, or if you don't have the full range of movement pictured, it is important to have patience with yourself. In time your stamina and flexibility will increase naturally, and it will become much easier to do each exercise for longer periods of time with a greater radius of movement. The rule is always to try to do a little more than you did the last time, if you can do it without increasing the strain on yourself.

There is almost no benefit from doing these exercises once or twice a week. They should be done at least five times a week at the beginning. Then, once you have achieved your desired results, you can reduce to a three-times-a-week maintenance program. Remember, results take time.

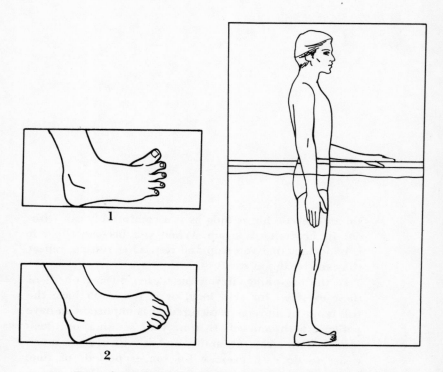

1

2

Exercise 16—To *relax, stretch* and *strengthen* the muscles surrounding your toe joints.

Stand in water to your waist as shown. Hold on to the side of the pool. Stretch out and open your toes as much as you can as shown in Figure 1. Then attempt to clench them together as shown in Figure 2. All opening and closing motions should feel as if you are *pushing* the water forward and backward. All movement should be *slow* and *gentle*.

If you intend to do the exercise at home, see the caution on page 84.

This exercise should be continued regardless of the advanced exercises you do.

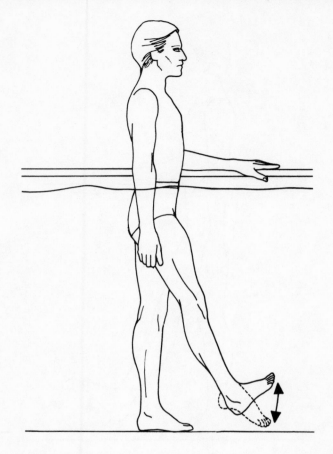

Exercise 17—To *relax, stretch* and *strengthen* the muscles surrounding your ankle joints.

Stand in water to your waist. Hold on to the side of pool. Raise and lower your foot below the ankle so that on the raising and lowering motions you feel as if you are *lifting* the water up and *pushing* the water down. All movement should be *slow* and *gentle*. (At no point should your toes touch the floor.)

If you intend to do the exercise at home, see the caution on page 84.

This exercise should be continued regardless of the advanced exercises you do, though you do get partial benefit from Exercises 26 and 33.

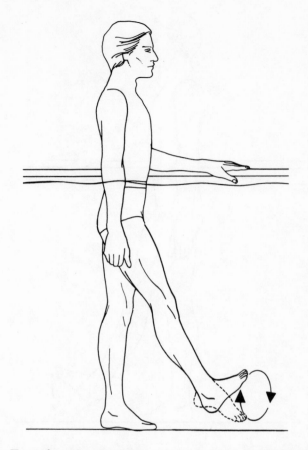

Exercise 18—Further to *relax, stretch* and *strengthen* the muscles surrounding your ankle joints.

Stand in water to your waist. Hold on to the side of the pool. Rotate your foot below the ankle so that you feel as if you are *pushing* the water around in a circular motion. The direction of rotation should be to the right for a period of time and then to the left for a period of time. All movement should take place in your foot below the ankle. Try not to move your upper leg around. All movement should be *slow* and *gentle*. (At no point should your toes touch the floor.)

This exercise should be continued regardless of the advanced exercises you do.

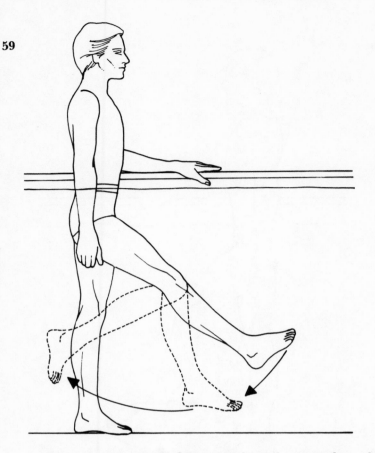

Exercise 19—To *relax, stretch* and *strengthen* the muscles surrounding your knee joints.

Stand in water to your waist. Hold on to the side of the pool. Move your leg below the knee forward and backward so that you feel as if you are *pushing* the water forward and backward. All movement should be *slow* and *gentle*.

If you also have ankle problems, do the exercise the way it is described in Exercise 26. If not, then continue this exercise the way it is described here regardless of the advanced exercises you do.

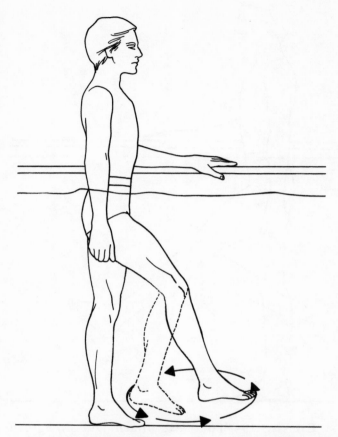

Exercise 20—Further to *relax, stretch* and *strengthen* the muscles surrounding your knee joints.

Stand in water to your waist. Hold on to the side of the pool. Rotate your leg below the knee in a circular motion. The direction of rotation should be to the left for a period of time and then to the right for a period of time. Try to make sure that most of the movement takes place in your leg below the knee. Try not to move your upper leg around. All lower-leg movement should feel as if you are *pushing* the water. All movement should be *slow* and *gentle*.

This exercise should be continued regardless of the advanced exercises you do.

Do an exercise for as long as you comfortably can without its becoming a strain. When you become tired, it is important that you stop and rest. After resting, repeat the exercise if you can.

In the beginning, if you can't even do any or all of these exercises for very long, or if you don't have the full range of movement pictured, it is important to have patience with yourself. In time your stamina and flexibility will increase naturally, and it will become much easier to do each exercise for longer periods of time with a greater radius of movement. The rule is always to try to do a little more than you did the last time, if you can do it without increasing the strain on yourself.

There is almost no benefit from doing these exercises once or twice a week. They should be done at least five times a week at the beginning. Then, once you have achieved your desired results, you can reduce to a three-times-a-week maintenance program. Remember, results take time.

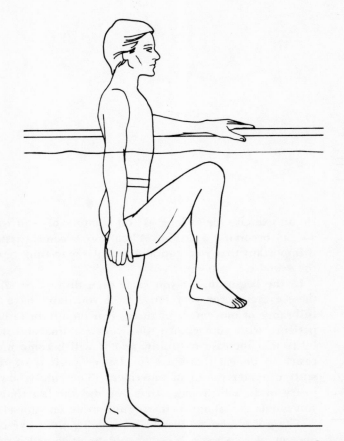

Exercise 21—To *relax, stretch* and *strengthen* the muscles surrounding your knee, hip and lower-back joints.

Stand in water to the middle of your rib cage. Hold on to side of pool. Raise and lower your knee so that the raising and lowering motions feel as if you are *lifting* the water up and *pushing* the water down. All movements should be *slow* and *gentle.*

This exercise should be replaced with Exercises 32 and 33 as soon as you are able to do so.

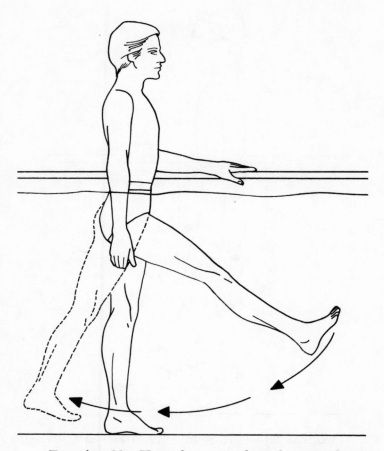

Exercise 22—To *relax, stretch* and *strengthen* the muscles surrounding your hip joints.

Stand in water to mid waist. Hold on to the side of the pool. Raise your leg forward, then lower it behind you, so that you feel as if you are *lifting* the water up and *pushing* the water down. All movement should be *slow* and *gentle*.

This exercise should be replaced with Exercises 32 and 33 as soon as you are able to do so.

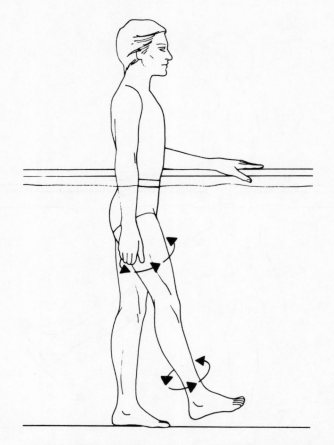

Exercise 23—Further to *relax, stretch* and *strengthen* the muscles surrounding your hip joints.

Stand in water to midwaist. Hold on to the side of the pool. Rotate your leg so that you feel as if you are *pushing* the water around in a narrow circular motion. The direction of rotation should be to the right for a period of time and then to the left for a period of time. All movement should be *slow* and *gentle*.

This exercise should be replaced with Exercises 32 and 33 as soon as you are able to do so.

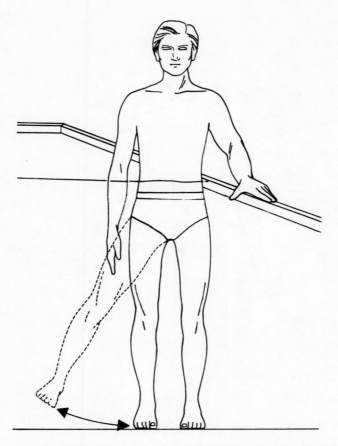

Exercise 24—Further to *relax, stretch* and *strengthen* the muscles surrounding your hip joints.

Stand in water to midwaist. Hold on to the side of the pool. Raise and lower your leg sideways so that on the raising and lowering motions you feel as if you are *lifting* the water up and *pushing* the water down. All movements should be *slow* and *gentle*.

This exercise should be replaced with Exercise 31 as soon as you are able to do so.

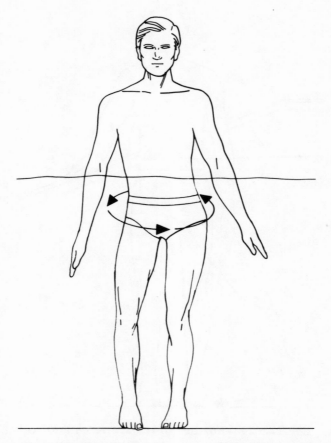

Exercise 25—To *relax, stretch* and *strengthen* the muscles surrounding your hip and lower-back joints.

Stand in water above your waist. Rotate your hips so that you feel as if you are *pushing* the water around in a circular motion. Rotation should be to the right for a period of time and then to the left for a period of time. All movements should be *slow* and *gentle*.

This exercise should be replaced with Exercises 34 and 35 as soon as you are able to do so.

Intermediate Exercises

Intermediate and advanced exercises are especially beneficial to people who have arthritis pains in more than one area. They enable you to exercise different areas at the same time and thus spend more time on each area. For instance, Exercise 27 combines three beginner's exercises for your wrist, elbow and shoulder. Instead of spending ten minutes exercising your wrist, ten minutes exercising your elbow, and ten minutes exercising your shoulder, you can exercise all three for thirty minutes by doing this one exercise for thirty minutes. Most other intermediate and advanced exercises don't look like exact combinations of beginner's exercises, but your benefits from doing them are the same as from doing groups of beginner's exercises.

You can start doing intermediate and advanced exercises whenever you feel you have improved to the point where you are able to do them.

The first time that you do Intermediate Exercises involving floating and/or swimming be sure that you do them in shallow water. Some people are less buoyant than others. You probably won't have any problem, but if you should have trouble staying afloat, do not strain yourself to do so. Do not thrash around trying to keep yourself from sinking. Instead, the next time you exercise, wear one of the swimming aids described in the chapter on Exercise Aids. If you need a swimming aid to exercise comfortably do not be embarrassed about it. Remember that its purpose is to help you help yourself.

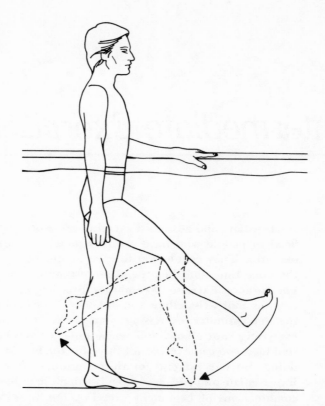

Exercise 26—To *relax, stretch* and *strengthen* the muscles surrounding your ankle and knee joints.

Stand in water to your waist. Hold on to the side of the pool. Start with your leg raised and your foot below the ankle arched as far back as it will comfortably go. Then start to move your leg below the knee backward, at the same time pushing downward with the ball of your foot. Move your leg below the knee as far back as it will comfortably go and your foot below the ankle as far down and back as it will comfortably go. On the return upward motion raise both your leg below the knee and your foot below the ankle. All movement should feel as if you are *pushing* and *lifting* the water. All movement should also be *slow* and *gentle*.

This exercise should be continued regardless of the advanced exercises you do.

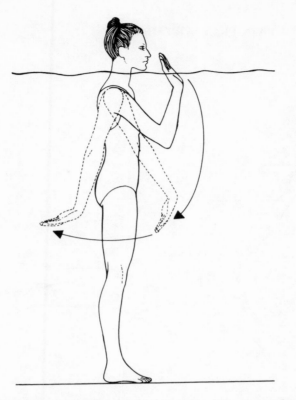

Exercise 27—To *relax, stretch* and *strengthen* the muscles surrounding your wrist, elbow and shoulder joints.

Stand in water above your shoulders. Raise your arm and bend back your wrist as if you were a waiter carrying a tray. Then push down with both your arm and your hand below the wrist. Move them both as far back and down as they will comfortably go. On the return upward motion raise both your arm and your hand below the wrist. All movement should be *slow* and *gentle*. On all raising and lowering motions, you should feel as if you are *lifting* the water up and *pushing* the water down.

This exercise should be replaced with Exercises 32 and 33 as soon as you are able to do so.

Exercise 28—Floating isn't really an exercise in and of itself, but it is an excellent way to relax while you are resting between exercises. When you are floating, the water nestles under every curve of your body, thus giving your body total support. The floating position is also the base from which you can do many beneficial back and neck exercises. When floating, it is important to keep your toes pointed, your chest out, your back arched and your head back. If you have trouble floating, try spreading your legs wider apart to give yourself additional balance. If doing that doesn't enable you to float effortlessly, then you should wear a swimming aid.

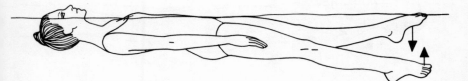

Exercise 29—To *relax, stretch* and *strengthen* the muscles surrounding your lower-back, hip, ankle and knee joints.

In the floating position, with your arms at your sides and your legs close together, raise and lower your legs with a kicking motion. Your range of motion should be approximately eight inches, with your toes rising no more than an inch or two out of the water. All raising and lowering motions should feel as if you are *lifting* the water up and *pushing* the water down. All movement should be *slow* and *gentle*.

This exercise should be replaced with Exercise 35 as soon as you are able to do so.

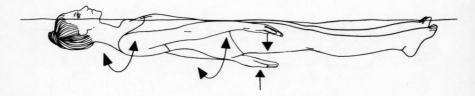

Exercise 30—To *relax, stretch* and *strengthen* the muscles surrounding your neck, shoulder and upper-back joints.

In the floating position, with your arms at your sides and your legs close together, raise and lower your arms. Your range of arm motion should be approximately eight inches, with your arms never rising above the water. Your right arm should move downward as your left arm moves upward. Then your right arm should move upward as your left arm moves downward. The alternate up and down arm movement should give a natural twisting motion to your shoulders and your hips. This twisting motion is so beneficial you should try to encourage and exaggerate it. All raising and lowering motions should feel as if you are *lifting* the water up and *pushing* the water down. All movement should be *slow* and *gentle*.

This exercise should be replaced with Exercise 35 as soon as you are able to do so.

Advanced Exercises

Don't worry if you can't do the advanced exercises exactly the way they are drawn. I've been doing them for years and I'm not sure I do them exactly the way they are drawn. Realize that you will benefit greatly from doing them approximately right. The important thing is that you start doing them and then attempt to improve gradually.

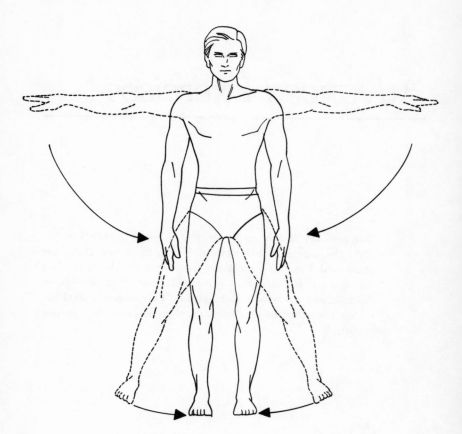

Exercise 31—*To relax, stretch* and *strengthen* the muscles surrounding your shoulder and hip joints.

In the floating position, with your arms and legs extended, bring your arms down to your sides and your legs together. All movement should feel as if you are *pushing* the water. All movement should also be *slow* and *gentle*.

Don't mistake this for a standing exercise. The illustration shows an overview looking down on someone floating in the water.

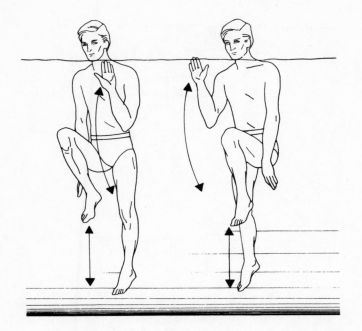

Exercise 32—To *relax, stretch* and *strengthen* the muscles surrounding your ankle, knee, hip, wrist, elbow, shoulder and lower-back joints.

This exercise is best done treading water in water over your head. If being in water over your head frightens you, start in water up to your chin. Raise and lower your knees, at the same time raising and lowering your arms below the elbows and hands below the wrist. Keep your wrists and ankles loose so that they get maximum up-and-down movement. The arm movement pictured here was purposely changed from the movement shown in swimming books, in order to give greater benefit to your wrists, elbows and shoulders. If you have lower-back pains, try to raise your knees as high as possible so as to achieve maximum stretching in your lower back. All movement should feel as if you are *lifting* the water up and *pushing* the water down. All movement should also be *slow* and *gentle*.

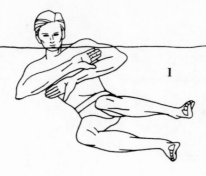

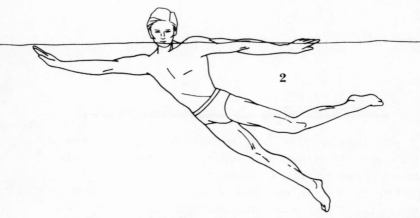

Exercise 33—To *relax, stretch* and *strengthen* the muscles surrounding your wrist, elbow, shoulder, ankle, knee and hip joints—doing the side stroke.

This isn't the classic side stroke as taught in swimming books, but doing it this way gives added benefit to your wrists and elbows. On your side, cross your arms parallel in front of you and bring your knees up toward your stomach. Move your arms and legs outward, with your last outward movement being felt in your wrists and ankles. All movement should feel as if you are *pushing* the water. All movement should also be *slow* and *gentle*.

I find this exercise to be so relaxing that I sometimes do it for a few minutes as a rest in between my other exercises.

Exercise 34—To *relax, stretch* and *strengthen* the muscles surrounding your neck, shoulder, back, hip, knee, ankle, elbow and wrist joints—doing the backstroke.

The twisting motion of the arms, the upper back and the hips pictured here is deliberately incorrect in terms of perfect swimming form (see below and pages 78–79). That is because your goal in doing this exercise is not to set Olympic swimming records but rather to provide maximum benefit to your neck, shoulders, back and hips. The additional twisting is the very thing that helps achieve that goal. It also enables you to move your elbows and wrists out of the water with minimum discomfort.

Figure 1: Start in the floating position with your hands by your sides and your legs close together.

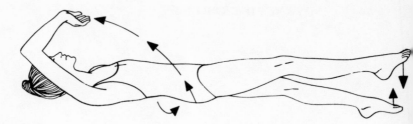

Figure 2: Start your kicking motion. Then raise your right arm backward so that the back of your right wrist passes over the left side of your head. On this raising motion you should both bend your elbow to the left and move your shoulder to the left. Your upper arm should almost touch your right ear as it passes near it. As your upper arm moves to the left your hips should twist slightly to the right.

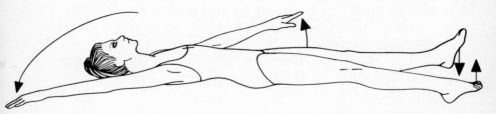

Figure 3: Continue kicking. Start raising your left hand out of the water. Rotate your right shoulder and wrist so that on your backward downward motion your palm faces the water and your fingers enter it first.

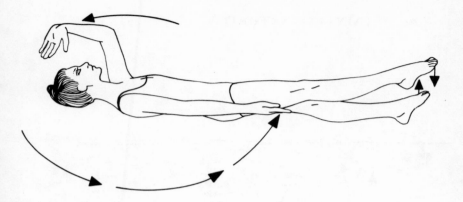

Figure 4: Continue kicking. Pass the back of your left wrist over the right side of your head. As your left arm moves up and to the right your hips should twist slightly to the left (not shown). Bring your right arm around through the water back to its original starting position. Your right arm is now in the starting position except that your palm is facing up instead of down. On each succeeding raising motion twist your wrist so that the back of your wrist can pass over the left side of your head.

All arm and leg movement should feel as if you are *pushing* and *lifting* the water. All movement should also be *slow* and *gentle*.

With this exercise, unlike Exercise 35, the more you twist your hips the more difficult it becomes to kick your feet. Both are beneficial, so try to find a happy medium between the two.

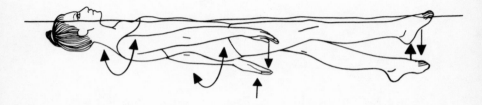

Exercise 35—To *relax, stretch* and *strengthen* the muscles surrounding your neck, shoulder, back, hip, knee and ankle joints.

In the floating position, with your hands by your sides and your legs close together, raise and lower your arms and legs. The range of motion of your arms and legs should be approximately eight inches, with your toes rising no more than an inch or two out of the water and your arms never leaving the water. Your right arm and right leg should move downward as your left arm and left leg move upward. Then your right arm and right leg should move upward as your left arm and left leg move downward. The alternate up and down movement should give a natural twisting motion to your hips and your shoulders. This twisting motion is so beneficial you should try to encourage and exaggerate it. All raising and lowering motions should feel as if you are *lifting* the water up and *pushing* the water down. All movement should also be *slow* and *gentle*.

The advanced exercises you find most beneficial will depend upon your particular condition. Personally, I find this exercise to be the most relaxing and pleasant one that I do. I use it to propel myself from one end of the pool to the other. I find this movement delightful.

ADVANCED-EXERCISE PROGRAMS

My own advanced-exercise program consists of forty-five minutes of alternating between Exercises 34 and 35. Then three minutes in the whirlpool, where I do the finger-flutter exercise, followed by forty-five more minutes of Exercises 34 and 35. In total, I usually do over 100 lengths of the pool, pausing only at the shallow end to clean my swimming goggles.

Occasionally, I also do sidestroke and water-treading exercises. I never do the crawl or the butterfly stroke, because doing them strains my neck and upper back. The reason for this is that in those strokes my neck and shoulders are above the water when I'm moving them.

I concentrate on Exercises 34 and 35 because they are the best advanced exercises for my condition. Between them, they are the best possible exercises for people whose main problems are hip, lower mid- and upper-back, shoulder and neck pains. If your main problems are with your wrists, elbows, ankles, knees, lower back and hips, the water-treading and sidestroke exercises are the ones you should spend most of your time doing.

In addition to the advanced exercises you do, if you have problems with your fingers or toes you will have to continue with the beginner's exercises for those conditions. Beginner's rotation exercises for ankles, knees, wrists and elbows should also be continued for a few minutes a day.

Even if you have arthritis pain in only one particular joint, it is still a good idea to spend some time doing a combination of advanced exercises. Any moderate exercise program is good for your general health, and this one in particular will prevent arthritis pain from developing in other parts of your body.

Whether you suffer from single or multiple arthritis pains, you should continue to gradually increase the time you spend exercising, until you reach the point where you are no longer in pain. From the time I started doing beginner's exercises ten minutes a day altogether, it took me nine months to work my way up to one and a half hours and total freedom from pain.

Everyone's condition is different. You might progress much faster than I did or much slower. Regardless, wait until you are at least one month without pain before reducing your exercise frequency to four times a week. After being without pain for an additional month, you can reduce to the three-times-a-week minimum.

If you wish to be without arthritis pain, you must continue with your water exercises three times a week for the rest of your life.

I have gotten to the point where I no longer look upon these exercises as exercise. Aside from the physical benefits I have derived from them, I find them so pleasurable and relaxing that I have come to enjoy them for their own sake. I hope that once you have recovered, you will come to enjoy them as much as I do.

SUPPLEMENTAL HOME EXERCISE

There are some exercises that can be done beneficially at home to supplement your pool exercises. Exercises 1, 2, 3 and 4 may be done in a sink filled with water. Sit or stand, whichever is most comfortable for you. Do them as many times a day as you are able to without straining yourself. If you find that sitting or standing this way out of the water strains any other part of your body, then confine your exercises to a pool. It is not worth it to worsen one condition to improve another.

Sink exercises plus Exercises 16, 17 and 18 may be done at home in the tub. I suggest you do them lying down so as not to chance slipping in the tub. If getting in and out of the tub is too much of a strain on your neck and back, do not

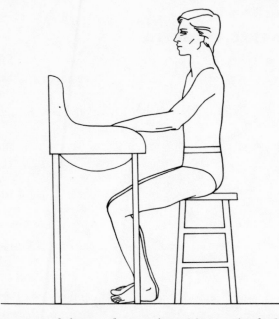

attempt any of these tub exercises. I know the feeling, because for years I was in too much pain to take a tub bath.

If at all possible, these home exercises should be done in addition to pool exercises, not instead of them. Remember, beneficial advanced exercises cannot be done in a sink or bathtub.

Exercising your hands and feet exclusively at home might not help. Your pain could be a referred pain. A referred pain is a pain felt one place but caused someplace else. It is possible that the pain in your hands is a referred pain caused by nerve pressure in your neck. The pain in your feet could also be a referred pain from your lower back. If that is the case, to get relief you must go to a pool and exercise the area that is causing your pain. For instance, if tense, tight and weak muscles press on nerve endings in your neck you might feel pain in your neck and also referred pain in your hands. If that is the case, then exercising your hands would not help your hands very much. To relieve both conditions you would have to go to a pool and exercise your neck.

Keep in mind that if you have pain in both your neck and your hands or lower back and feet one pain may be causing the other. If you have pain only in your hands or feet it is much less likely but still possible that the pain you feel is a referred pain. If you don't want to worry about referred pain, go to a pool and work up to doing advanced exercises.

Exercise Aids

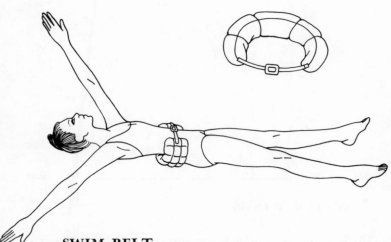

SWIM BELT

If you are unable to float because you aren't naturally buoyant, this device will enable you to do so. Buckle the swim
belt in front, just below your ribs. Relax and lie back on the
water. You'll be amazed how easy it is to float. With the aid
of a swim belt, you'll be able to participate in all the beneficial previously described exercises that start from the floating position.

If the pool you go to has any sort of program for teaching
swimming, they probably have swim belts available without
charge. Ask about them. If they are not available at your
pool, they can be purchased at well-stocked sporting-goods
stores.

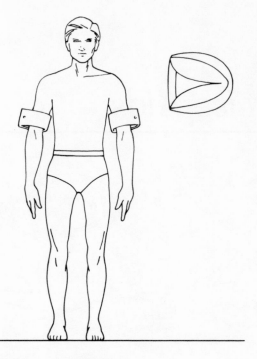

WATER WINGS

This is an equally effective swimming aid of different design. Even though it is worn only on the upper arms it provides support for the entire body. If you aren't naturally buoyant or are afraid of the water these water wings will enable you to benefit from doing intermediate and advanced exercises that require the ability to float or swim.

Each wing has a flat side that is worn inward to allow for natural arm movement.

This set of two inflatable water wings comes packaged with instructions and retails for about four dollars.

If you want this type of swimming aid show this picture to your local sporting-goods store and ask about it. If that doesn't work, drop me a note in care of my publisher and I'll be glad to supply a distributor's name.

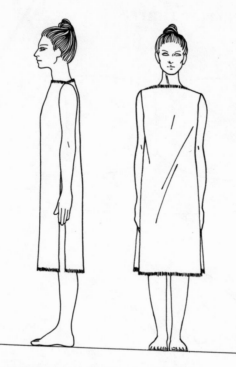

TURKISH-TOWEL TABARD

For use in the locker room and going to and from the sauna and the shower in order to protect yourself from drafts, here is something you can put together yourself that is lighter to carry than a bathrobe and easier to put on.

To Make: Take two turkish bath towels and join two of the narrow ends, making sure that you leave an opening for your head to slide through easily.

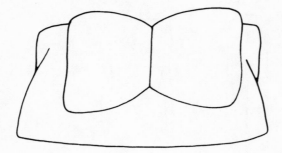

HOME-MADE CERVICAL PILLOW

If you need neck support when you are lying in bed, here is a tip that will save you the expense of buying a cervical pillow. Wrap ½ inch of elastic tightly around the middle of a regular pillow. Sew the ends of the elastic together. On top of another regular pillow, stand this pillow up on one of its longer sides and place your neck in the center of the standing pillow. I have found this to give me better neck support than any cervical pillow that I ever purchased in a surgical-supply store.

My Life After

These pictures indicate, I hope, that I am a real person. I don't have before-and-after pictures, because "before" I didn't know there was going to be an "after." When I was sick and in pain I looked as bad on the outside as I felt on the inside and I wouldn't allow pictures of myself to be taken. All I can tell you is that people tell me that I look ten years younger now than I did five years ago.

Pain relief was the primary purpose of my special water exercise program. An unlooked-for bonus is that in the last few years I've lost twenty pounds without dieting, firmed up my body and tremendously increased my energy level. I have also lowered both my pulse rate and my blood pressure.

I may be a little vain about my improvement, but the important thing is that my achievement is unique only because you haven't yet duplicated it. What I did you can do.

GENERAL COMMENTS ON MY RECOVERY

1. The feeling of accomplishment I have about my physical improvement makes me feel as if I were walking on water instead of exercising in water. Thinking about how crippled I was and how much better I am now because of my

own efforts gives me a tremendous feeling of satisfaction and self-worth.

2. Everyone living on this earth has real and imagined problems that bother them. When mine start to get me down, I think about how much pain I used to be in, and that helps put whatever is bothering me in perspective.

3. Most drugs have unpleasant side effects. The pleasant side effects from my water exercises are that I've lost weight, firmed up and improved my figure and increased my general energy level. One can't imagine the change in my attitude toward my body. I used to be so ashamed of my appearance, and now I feel so proud when the compliments roll in on how fit I look and how much stamina and endurance I now possess.

4. The important thing about my special water exercise program is that it has enabled me to once again lead a normal functioning life. When I was sick, the acts of cooking, cleaning, walking, getting in and out of a car all caused me additional pain. Almost anything that required movement hurt me to one degree or another. Now, as long as I keep up with my water exercises, I can carry on all normal activities without any pain whatsoever.

5. When my arthritis first became serious, in addition to going to doctors, one of the first things I did was buy a book about arthritis. It took the doctor who wrote the book 170 pages to say "Drink a lot of water, eat fruits and leafy green vegetables and think happy thoughts and your arthritis will go away." It probably would have gone away if I had followed his advice and also coincidentally had a natural remission.

Before writing this book, I went to the library and read every book I could about arthritis to see if anyone else had discovered the benefits of water exercises. What I found amazed me. There were doctors saying that diet was the answer. Other doctors were saying not only that diet wasn't the answer, but that some of the diets were outright frauds.

One doctor said massage was good for you, while another said it was harmful. The one I liked best was the doctor with a diagram of a neck exercise that could have easily killed a person with a neck a lot stronger than mine. The only reference I found to water treatment was the hospital use of the Hubbard Tank. This was said to be very beneficial to severely crippled arthritics.

      6. I have heard many strange diets for arthritis. They range from adding zinc to your diet to drinking cod-liver oil to eating alfalfa seeds. According to the Arthritis Foundation, all of these exotic diets are just so much nonsense. The only type of diet they recommend is a normal well-balanced diet that should be eaten by everyone, whether they have arthritis or not.

My own experience confirms the opinion of the Arthritis Foundation. I have been eating the same foods during the period before I became sick, during the time I suffered most from arthritis and during my recovery. In those ten years, my condition changed drastically, but my diet remained the same.

      7. One of the reasons people believe in quack cures is that at times they appear to work. People don't realize, though, that it is not the effectiveness of the "cure" that's helping them but rather that they are having a natural remission from their arthritis. When and if these remissions occur, they occur regardless of the "cure," not because of it.

It is unrealistic to expect a treatment to eliminate your pain unless that treatment effectively treats the cause of your pain.

      8. When I was sick and in pain I couldn't stand the winter cold in New York. No matter how warmly I dressed, I felt stiffer and in more pain whenever I ventured outside. Now, as long as I dress warmly, the cold has no effect on me whatsoever.

      9. When my hands were crippled, I had to shop for dresses that zipped down the front and bras that hooked in

front. Now that I'm better, it is such a pleasure to look for clothes, worrying only if they are attractive, not whether I'm able to put them on or not.

10. I'll never forget when I was sick, bursting into a scream at some poor man who was just trying to be friendly. Upon being introduced, he shook hands with me before I could stop him. The pain in my hand was unbelievable, and his embarrassment at my reaction was even worse. I think of that incident now whenever I painlessly shake hands with new acquaintances.

11. Now that I'm no longer suffering, I have a much more positive outlook on life. I have a patience for people and an interest in doing things that I had found impossible when I was so involved in my own pain.

12. I've come a long way in my recovery. From not being able to hold a pen without pain, to being able to hold up a falling man. A friend of mine started to black out in midsentence as we were standing beside the pool. I watched in horror as he started to fall slowly backward, head first, toward the tile floor. I grabbed him just in time with both my hands on his right arm, then quickly put my leg under him so that I could slide him to the floor without breaking his head. The strength of my grip on his arm was so great that he had ten black-and-blue marks that lasted for three weeks.

I hate to think what would have happened to this 185-pound man if my exercises hadn't strengthened my body to the point where I was able to help him.

13. To maintain my condition I only have to exercise three times a week, but when I have the benefit of a convenient pool I'll gladly swim seven days a week. When I find myself in a relatively empty pool I take advantage of the situation and swim for two or two and a half hours instead of my normal one and a half hours. I do this additional swimming because I really enjoy it.

After you have achieved your desired results you don't

necessarily have to reduce to a three-times-a-week maintenance program. If you have the time and you enjoy doing
them, by all means continue your water exercises up to
seven days a week for as many hours as you find pleasurable.

14. I don't want you to think that I've accomplished
what I have because I'm some sort of superathlete. Before
I started my special water exercise program I hadn't exercised in forty years and I was additionally in a great deal of
pain. I didn't start swimming 100 lengths of the pool. When
I started I couldn't do one length. Initially I had to work
myself up to doing one width of the pool. All improvement
just followed in natural slow progression. Once you start your
program you'll see for yourself how easy this really is.

15. When you are doing exercise to eliminate arthritis pain, the work ethic prevails. The more you do, the more
you achieve. My special water exercise program enables you
to achieve more because it enables you to do more. If you
were doing land exercise, you would have to torture yourself to build up to doing ten exercise repetitions. Once the
pain factor is removed by exercising in water, there is almost
no limit to the number of repetitions you can gradually build
up to doing.

During each maintenance session I do at least fifty lengths
of the pool of Exercise 34 and at least fifty additional lengths
of Exercise 35. In one length of doing Exercise 34 my arms,
legs, shoulders and hips are each moved eight times. In one
length of doing Exercise 35 my arms, legs, shoulders and hips
are each moved forty-four times. In one hour-and-a-half session this adds up to moving each arm, leg, shoulder and hip
2,600 times.

These numbers shouldn't intimidate you. They should encourage you. Your buildup will be so gradual you won't
realize you're doing it until you've done it. In fact, I had
no idea I did so much until I counted for the purpose of
writing this book. At any rate, swimming slowly on your
back is effortless and pleasurable, not tortured and painful.

When you compare the benefit derived from doing ten pain-ful repetitions with the benefit derived from doing 2,600 painless ones, you can understand why my special water exer-cise program is such a dramatic advance in the treatment of arthritis pain.

16. Throughout most of this book, I may sound self-inflated, but I don't think of myself as a heroine. I was terri-fied of my water exercises before I tried them, but I was even more terrified of becoming a complete cripple. So I tried.

The first time I ever went into a whirlpool, it took me seven days to get in. When I was told the temperature was 105 degrees, I was understandably wary. I decided to try it gradually. The whirlpool had four steps and I went in one step a day. Then I sat one minute the first day, two minutes the second day and finally three minutes the third day. It took me a week to finish a three-minute session. That's the way I've accomplished most of the things I've done. Nothing heroic, just slow, steady perseverance.

Conclusion

So far, this book has been about my problems with arthritis, my program for arthritis, and my recommending that program to you. I'm going to conclude with the comments of some people who have already followed my recommendations. These women are patients of Dr. Jagendorf. He sent them to me to show them how to alleviate their arthritis pain. They follow the same program that I have described to you.

"Before starting Dvera's program I suffered from low back pain on and off for fifteen or twenty years. I was diagnosed as having osteoarthritis and osteoporosis. At times my pain was so severe that it totally incapacitated me. The result of my following Dvera's program is that I no longer experience recurrent back pain. A pinched nerve that I suffered from is also much better. Now I can cook, clean, market, walk, dance and swim—all without pain. I feel marvelous."

Ann Goldstein
Brooklyn, New York

"Being on Dvera's program has helped me tremendously. For two years I had slight pain in my fingers and bad pain in the back of my neck. I couldn't turn my head without hurting myself. I also suffered for fifty years from pain in my knee. In the last few of those years the pain kept getting worse. Now I am in no pain at all and, more than that, I feel great. Each day after swimming I have more energy than before I started. Dvera's program is terrific. I wish I had known about it years ago."

Jean Kaufman
Brooklyn, New York

It gives me great satisfaction to know that my program is helping to change lives for the better. My experience working with other arthritics has further confirmed my conviction that once this program becomes known it will help change millions of lives for the better.

Having been a sufferer from arthritis I have empathy for my fellow sufferers. If you want to, please write to me in care of my publishers. I'm interested in your comments about my book and, more importantly, the progress of your recovery.

GOOD LUCK AND GOOD HEALTH!